How to ACE your EXAMS

For Mum, Dad and Phil, who taught me that being nice
and working hard is the way to go about things,
and who are always there unconditionally.

For Liv, T and Margs, who I hope read this and benefit
from it (despite it being written by their dad).

And for Laura, who is the best person in the world.

First published in Great Britain in 2024 by Wren & Rook

ISBN: 978 1 5263 6408 1

3 5 7 9 10 8 6 4 2

MIX
Paper | Supporting
responsible forestry
FSC
www.fsc.org   FSC® C104740

Wren & Rook
An imprint of
Hachette Children's Group
Part of Hodder & Stoughton
Carmelite House
50 Victoria Embankment
London EC4Y 0DZ

An Hachette UK Company
www.hachette.co.uk
www.hachettechildrens.co.uk

Printed and bound in Great Britain by Clays Ltd, Elcograf S.p.A.

The nation's favourite head teacher
MATTHEW BURTON

How to ACE your EXAMS

wren &rook

CONTENTS

INTRODUCTION

You wake up early — wide-eyed, completely bolt upright. No fumbling in the dark for the snooze button or lazily giving yourself *'just five more minutes'*. For a moment, there's the usual question of, *'Ahh, what am I doing today?'* before you remember. **It's exam season. GAH.**

You overpour milk on to your cereal, while your mind flicks through those key dates and formulae you've been wrestling with for months. You get dressed in your uniform (putting your left sock on first for good luck) and recite a couple of lines of poetry you might just need to quote. You begin the slow journey to school, taking every possible second you can to check those revision cards.

When you arrive, you look across the ocean of uniform-clad nervousness descending on the school hall. It's a feeling that everyone has. It's unmistakeable. **Exam nerves.** So much worry and so much anxiety. Have I remembered this? Did I revise enough of that? What if that dreaded question comes up?

But — it doesn't have to be like that. This book is going to get you so prepped and ready you'll be confident of doing a smashing job from the first minute of your first exam to the start of that long, golden summer. And when you tear open that brown envelope to reveal your results, you'll realise it was worth all the hard graft along the way.

You're going to find **twenty-five top tips and techniques** to help you to rinse that **revision**, smash those **studies**, handle that **homework** and **ace your exams**. This book alone can't guarantee your exams will fly phenomenally, but it can help you to structure your approach to them, so that the minute you're in that exam hall, you can enter with your head held high, ready to give it everything.

So, in that moment, remember: You've worked for it. You've planned for it. You're ready for it. Some of this will go well; some of it won't. But you'll handle it, because you have a plan. So take deep breaths in and deep breaths out.

ARE YOU READY? IT'S TIME TO BEGIN. GOOD LUCK!

PART ONE

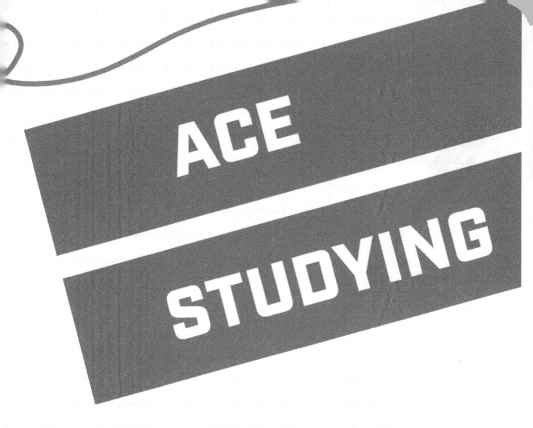

ACE STUDYING

Whether you're two years away from your exams or two months away, there are things you can do to help you study. From **preparing** right and getting into a **routine** to mastering your **subjects** and staying **motivated**, laying down the foundations of your **revision** and **understanding why** you are doing what you are doing is key.

1

SET GREAT GOALS

Having a strong idea of what you want helps you plan a route towards getting there *and* keeps you motivated along the way. **Goal-setting** is scientifically linked to better performance and increased self-confidence, which is exactly what you need when you are studying for your exams.

SHORT, MEDIUM AND LONG

Goals come in different sizes. Your ultimate destination is your **long-term goal**, and it's different for everyone. You might want to be a teacher, you might want to run your family's business or you might even want to be the next prime minister!

Along the way, you're going to need a variety of **short-term** and **medium-term goals**. These are things that are going to act as stepping stones to larger success. It helps to work backwards from the ultimate goal, so you can work out what you need to do to get there.

FOR EXAMPLE:

LONG-TERM GOAL:
- Become a qualified English teacher working in a secondary school

MEDIUM-TERM GOALS:
- Complete an undergraduate degree
- Complete teacher training
- Gain in-class work experience

SHORT-TERM GOALS:
- Investigate the routes into teaching and what I need to do to get there
- Talk to teachers about my aims
- Pass my exams

Now, your turn . . . Get your hands on an A3 piece of paper, or the biggest you can find, and write out your core, long-term goal right in the middle of it, in a circle. Around that core goal, place medium- and short-term goals that are going to help you get there. **What will acing your exams help you to do in the future?**

Stick your goal up on your wall and use it to motivate yourself when you're studying.

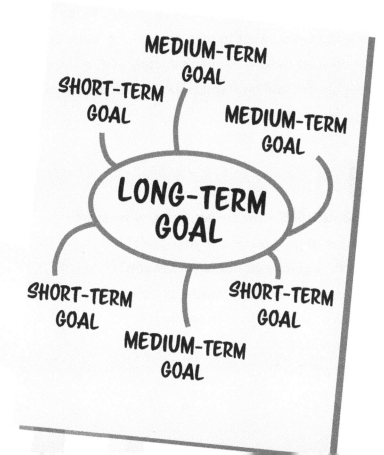

GET SMART

If you want to get more out of your goals, try to make them **SMART**. (Well, it beats them being STUPID, right?) OK, not that kind of SMART. I mean SMART as in:

S

Specific: Really try to hone in on your goal. It's one thing to say you want to be a doctor long-term, but do you want to be a children's doctor, a GP, a surgeon? Being specific will help you work out precisely what steps you need to take.

M

Measurable: How are you going to measure whether or not you've met your goals? Is it by getting certain grades in your exams? If so, they will help you measure success and pivot accordingly if things are not quite up to scratch.

A

Achievable: Your short-term goal might be to learn all the themes, plot devices, character motivations and important quotes from *Macbeth*, all in the space of one day. But hold on a minute — is that achievable? Be realistic about your goals — **you're only human!** (Aren't you?)

R

Relevant: Make sure the actions you are taking are relevant to your goals. Reading your favourite novel might feel like a nice way to get in the zone for your English exam, but are you sure that is relevant?

T

Time-bound: Give yourself a deadline. Without a clear sense of when you want to achieve your goals by, you can end up putting them off altogether.

Setting goals is about setting yourself up for success – it's a crucial tool for acing those exams. You need to know where you're going before you can get there.

2

GET IN THE
HABIT

To ace exams, you need to get into **good habits**, so it's useful to know how habits form in the first place. Let's start with an example of a *bad* one: the habit of scrolling endlessly on your phone. (Something that pretty much EVERYONE has a problem with.)

- First, there's the **cue**: this is the thing that makes you think about your phone in the first place. For example, when a notification goes off.

- Then, there's the **craving**: this is your body's excitement and anticipation before picking up the phone.

- This is followed by the **response**: the action you take – i.e. grabbing your phone and scrolling for hours!

- Finally, there's the **reward**: that's the lovely warm fuzzy feeling you get – provided by the neurotransmitter **dopamine** – when you get likes on social media or a message from a friend.

The quicker you get to the reward bit, the more likely it is your brain is going to want to stick to that habit. You can see how that might make scrolling on your phone a really sticky habit. Good habits, like knuckling down to your studies, are a lot harder to stick to. They mostly happen because you recognise you want to

MAKE A POSITIVE CHANGE TO YOUR BEHAVIOUR.

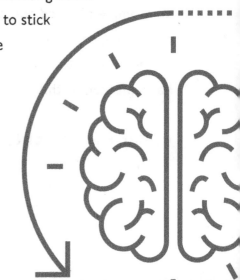

To develop good habits, follow these five steps:

STEP 1: BE POSITIVE

Positive thinking actively reduces stress and can help dispel anxiety. If you look at new study habits positively, as ways to help **Future You** achieve your long-term goals, then it becomes much easier to develop them.

STEP 2: START SMALL

You don't have to develop amazing study habits overnight. Start small. Spending five minutes catching up on your notes before breakfast every other day one week could become ten minutes the next, and then fifteen after that.

STEP 3: MAGNETISE!

Add a habit to another habit you already do by **magnitising** it. For example, you brush your teeth every morning, right? Well, can you magnetise that activity by listening to a Spanish podcast, to help boost your language learning at the same time? **Forming new habits** is easier when you're building on top of things your brain **does routinely** anyway.

 ## STEP 4: BE FLEXIBLE

Look, sometimes you'll wake up in the morning and feel rubbish. Suddenly that habit of doing fifteen minutes of English studies before breakfast is hard to stick to. If you need to, change it up. Move it to the end of the day. **Being flexible is not being a failure.**

 ## STEP 5: MAKE IT FUN

Try listening to music to keep things engaging – classical music has been linked to **stimulating brain waves**, which activates memory. Or, if that's not your bag, turn studying into a game. Plan out mini-rewards after each 'level' or module you complete over the weeks and months, until you reach the ultimate boss – your exams!

LOOK TO IMPROVE

It's important to know if your current study habits are working for you. Reflect on them using the **embed, restart and begin method.**

EMBED

This is when you want to make sure you keep doing an action or habit that is valuable and working. Maybe you usually work best in the morning and can see the positive effects it has on your studies – now you need to **embed** it, making sure that the habit is built solidly into your routine. *(Maybe you scroll on your phone for hours on end – that habit is NOT one you want to embed.)*

RESTART

This is when you used to take a specific action, but it just felt like such an effort, so you stopped. Maybe you were in the habit of doing all your homework the night you got it, but other stuff seemed much more interesting and started getting in the way. If it was working, it might be time to **restart.**

BEGIN

This is when you've always wanted to start doing a certain action, but have never known quite how to. This is sometimes the most difficult, because starting a new habit or routine isn't easy. That's not to say you shouldn't do it – **YOU SHOULD!** When is a better time to start doing something than when you are studying for your exams? Hint: there isn't one!

SMALL STEPS

If forming good habits seems like a gigantic mountain to climb, think about the science of **small steps.** This is the idea that by making consistent, small improvements to the things we're doing, rather than going from 0 to 100 in the blink of an eye, we can get amazing results.

Imagine you're building a house and you're adding just one brick a day. OK – that's going to take a while. But guess what – eventually you're going to have solid foundations, and after that, a house! What's going to happen if you don't add a brick every day, or worse, you keep taking bricks away? No house for you!

Think about how you can add a brick a day to the house of your studies. For example:

- Find the perfect, quiet place where you can work in peace
- Set study goals for each session
- Space out your studying so it doesn't overwhelm you

THE HABITS YOU FORM ARE SO IMPORTANT.

Keep building on them and you'll have a **solid foundation** for acing your exams.

3

KNOW YOURSELF NOW

OK, **this sounds deep.** But in order to ace your studies — and therefore your exams — you have to know yourself, and you have to do it NOW! Don't worry, you don't have to go on some fancy spiritual retreat — all you need to know is: what you're **good at** and what you're **not good at**.

Research shows that identifying our strengths and weaknesses makes us more confident and creative. It's vital for identifying gaps in our knowledge.

So, which one of these best describes you?

I'M AN 'I-DON'T-PARTICULARLY-CARE-R'

Do you think there's no point studying because it won't do any good? Does that glass of water on the side appear to be half empty (instead of half full)? Do you simply not care?

If this is you – head right back to chapter 1 and set some goals. It might be you've never really thought of it before, but goals will give you concrete reasons for wanting to do well in your exams. They are scientifically proven to be linked with higher motivation and self-esteem – goals literally make you care!

I'M A WORRIER

If you're consumed by a sense of complete dread and fear at what's coming, and it makes you feel physically sick, you're a worrier. A level of nervousness is normal – after all, these are important exams at an important time – but letting it take over will stop you achieving your best.

If your worries are extreme and uncontrollable, ask for some help from home, school or the GP. If they're manageable – and, remember, lots of worries are and everyone will feel some worry – then focus on planning well, developing healthy habits, rewarding yourself, taking rest and visualising success. This can go a long way to taking the edge off that panic. (To learn how to visualise success and take time out, turn to pages 54 and 113.)

I'M A BIT DISORGANISED

If your bag's at your friend's house and your pencil case is at school, while your PE kit lives in your locker (stinking) and your homework occasionally gets done but not always, then you could be someone who is a bit disorganised.

Get organised by:

- Making lists of the subjects and topics you need to cover. Use the syllabus and ask your teacher if you're unsure
- Prioritise areas you know you need to strengthen
- Use calendars and planners to mark key dates and help plan your time
- Keep a course binder of all the material you will need for revision
- Write a study checklist, ticking off each item as you hit important milestones

I'M A CONFIDENT, CALM CHARACTER

You know it's going to be hard work and tough going, but you're ready for it. You're happy that you've done what you can to prepare yourself for this and you feel like you'll hit those exams at the right time.

If this fits the bill for you, well done . . . so far! Having confidence in your abilities has been proven to help people face difficult challenges and exert greater control over tricky situations. However, don't let confidence slip into complacency – keep your eyes on the prize!

I'M A CHANCER

Have you decided that exam season might be fine or that it might not be, but either way it's not going to affect what you do? Are you the type of person who'd rather ignore the stuff your classmates and friends are doing and just think, 'Well, it'll go how it'll go; there's not much I can do about it'?

If that's you, you need to find your 'why?'. This could be that:

- You want to make someone proud
- You want to prove you can smash these exams
- You want to take the first step on the road to a career of your dreams

If so, get yourself back to chapter 1 and work on those goals. Being clear about what you hope to get from these exams is key to success.

Whatever the why is, find it. Once you've found it, use it as motivation to take as many elements of chance out of your exams as possible. Remember — knowing why you're doing something gives you motivation. Motivation, once you act on it, is scientifically proven to give your brain that lovely fuzzy reward feeling, courtesy of the neurotransmitter dopamine.

Be honest about which type of person you identify with the most. You've got time to do something about it and it could make a real difference as you naturally work out what you do well and what you shy away from.

BEFORE YOU KNOW IT, YOU'LL BE AN, EXAM-SMASHING MACHINE!

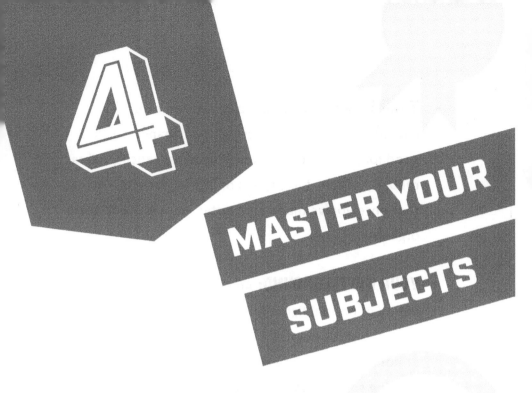

4

MASTER YOUR SUBJECTS

You're going into battle, facing stiff opposition in the form of the list of subjects you're taking and the topics you're going to need to conquer. To succeed, you'll need:

- **YOUR TROOPS:** Otherwise known as books, revision notes and tons of helpful websites. There are loads of amazing resources online that can help you master any subject and take out the enemy. Ask your teachers which ones they recommend for their specific subject.

- **YOUR WEAPONS:** Notebooks, revision cards, colourful sticky notes — basically, any paper which is good for jotting down notes. Plus pens, pencils, rulers, rubbers, folders, files, boxes or plastic pockets — so that once you've made your notes, you can keep them organised.

- **YOUR BATTLEGROUND:** An uncluttered desk, with plenty of natural light. This might not always be easy to find, but it's helpful if you can. If there's no space at home, try your local library. They are always quiet, calming spaces and the librarians will be happy to have you!

But that's not all. To master your subject, you also need to assess your current skill level. Why not see where you are on the

SLIDING SCALE OF SUBJECT SPICINESS!

MILD: This subject is doable. Without being complacent, you've got this one!

LIGHT SPICE: Zingy, but manageable. A bit of a step up in terms of difficulty level, but reasonable. This subject keeps you your toes, but it's OK.

MEDIUM: A little bit eye-watery. This subject makes you sweat as you take on lots of new information.

HOT: You're not a giver-upper, but this one is getting HOT! Despite gulping down bottles of water and bathing yourself in metaphorical yoghurt, there's loads of difficult information, and it doesn't always feel like it's linked together.

OFF THE SCALE SPICY HOT HOT HOT! SEND THIS BACK TO THE KITCHEN, WAITER! Wow. Your forehead's sweaty, you need to loosen your collar and shift your tie to one side. This is the subject that, despite knowing it's important, you really struggle with.

Try it yourself: Grab a piece of paper and draw a table with five columns. Where do your subjects fall on the level of spiciness?

NOW YOU KNOW WHAT'S OFF-THE-SCALE SPICY, YOU KNOW WHERE YOU NEED TO SPEND THE MOST TIME, AND YOU CAN ENJOY REVISING THOSE MILDER SUBJECTS WITHOUT TOO MUCH STRESS.

FACE FACTS

We all have those subjects we say we hate. However, the reality is that you probably don't hate them, you just find them challenging. To master your subjects, **ask for help** from those around you, and don't shy away from after-school sessions, study lunchtimes or any other help that's offered. If you ignore spicy subjects, they won't simply vanish – they'll get worse.

The best thing I ever did was give my notes to my mum and dad. Not so I could demonstrate just how difficult the subject was, but so they could fire random questions at me for a few minutes at a time, a few times every day. You could involve the people around you to feel like your squad are helping you to master the subject too. I'm not sure what my dad ever did with the knowledge about square roots and the past tense of the French verb 'jouer', but I'm sure it helped him in some way!

ELABORATE, DON'T COMPLICATE

To master your subjects, use elaborative interrogation, i.e. **ask why** and **how**. For example, you could study a fact, such as:

Photosynthesis is the process by which plants use sunlight, water and CO_2 to create energy and oxygen.

But to really embed that learning, try asking yourself:

> **How** does photosynthesis produce energy for a plant?
>
> **Why** is sunlight crucial for plant growth?
>
> **Where** inside the plant does photosynthesis occur? And **when?**

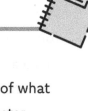

Asking **how** and **why** questions forces you to interrogate your learning, gets under the bonnet of what you know and what you don't, and helps you master topics rather than relying on surface-level knowledge. Try it yourself!

FIND WHAT WORKS FOR YOU

Not everyone learns in the same way — some people can't get enough of burying their heads in a book and soaking up all the info they can. Others need visual aids, or they learn best by listening, watching videos or chatting things through with others. Experiment with different methods, and then . . .

PRACTISE! WHEN WE REPEAT ACTIVITIES, WE ARE ACTIVELY STRENGTHENING THE CONNECTIONS BETWEEN NEURONS IN THE BRAIN. PATHWAYS ARE BEING LAID DOWN, WHICH WILL BECOME SUPERHIGHWAYS OF INFORMATION THAT MAKE FACTS QUICKER TO RECALL.

5

BE QUEEN (OR KING!) OF ROUTINE

Routines are there to help streamline most of the functional things you do **day-to-day,** and the positive effects of them are rooted in science. The more the brain can predict what's going to happen, the more it's able to free up mental space for other things, **such as studying!**

Routines are built upon clear goals (which you should already have set), **good habits** (which you've already learnt how to form) and **knowing what kind of studier you are** (which you've already established). Done right, routines help maximise your learning. So let's make you a routine queen (or king — which, I'm sorry, just doesn't rhyme as well)!

STRUCTURE

First things first, you need a plan. Look at your week ahead and determine what you're going to study and when. Are Mondays set aside for history and Thursdays for maths? Create a visual schedule like the one on the opposite page to help keep your studies on track during the week.

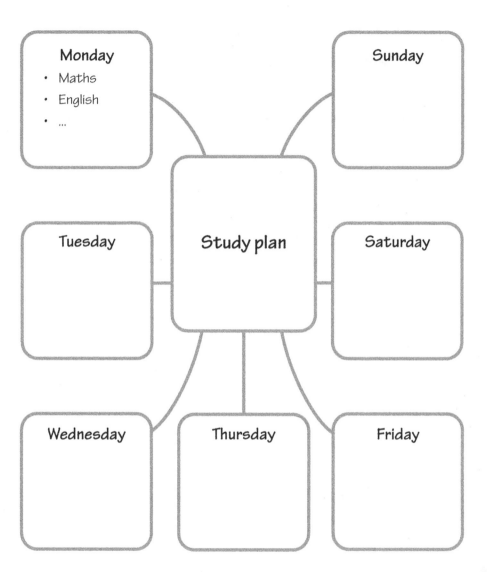

Monday
- Maths
- English
- ...

Sunday

Tuesday

Study plan

Saturday

Wednesday

Thursday

Friday

Your **schedule** might look very different if you're trying to revise at the same time as having lessons. If so, block out the time you need for those, as well as time for rest, and see what you have left to work with.

INTERVAL CHUNKS

When it comes to the nitty-gritty of study sessions, there are time management methods you can use to make the best of your schedule.

You might have a morning of study dedicated to maths. But try breaking up that study session into four **bite-size chunks of roughly thirty minutes**, then having **ten-minute breaks in between**.

For example:

Chunk one: Thirty minutes of algebra
Ten-minute break

Chunk two: Thirty minutes of fractions
Ten-minute break

Chunk three: Thirty minutes of probability
Ten-minute break

Chunk four: Thirty minutes of quadratic equations

Finally, finish with a longer break of twenty to thirty minutes.

Each chunk should be short enough to keep your brain focused on one task, before it starts daydreaming about something else entirely. And the mini-breaks in between are the perfect chance to rehydrate and refocus. Phew!

STEPPING STONES

Break tasks up into smaller pieces and use each one as an achievable milestone. You could write them out as a list and tick them off, or put them all in a grid that you colour in once you've completed the task.

Nothing is more satisfying than tracking progress and **seeing how far you've come**.

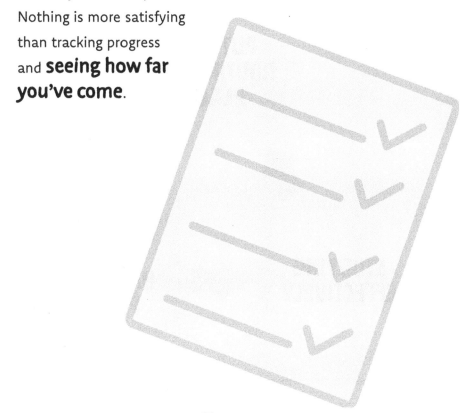

45

THE HAPPY STUDY CYCLE

When it comes to studying, think about this:

Putting routines in place is going to give you the opportunity to put your good habits into practice.

Putting your good habits into practice is going to help you study effectively.

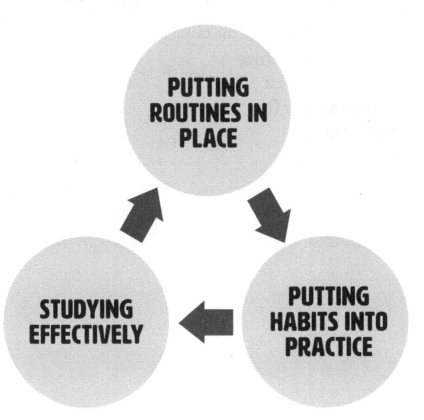

Studying effectively will help you figure out what you still need to work on, which will help you improve your routine, allowing you to change things up if they're getting stale.

Each element of the cycle feeds into the next one, creating a happy study cycle. It'll be a challenge to get started, just like any change to your life takes time to get comfortable with. But once you're up and running, your brain will have much more freed-up space in its working memory — and you'll be queen (or king!) of your routine.

RULE WELL!

6

BE A MOTIVATION MONSTER!

Motivation is KEY to acing your exams. It is proven to play a part in everything from your emotional wellbeing to your energy levels. When times are tough, use these motivational techniques to keep motivation **high** and become an exam-chomping, study-smashing **MOTIVATION MONSTER!**

SHARE YOUR PROBLEMS

Very often, a problem shared feels so much better. Whether it's a parent, a step-parent, a carer, a teacher, a dinner lady or anyone else whose **advice** you want, it doesn't matter. It just needs to be someone you can be honest with, value the wisdom of and feel comfortable with. Finding those mentors to 'bounce' your problems off isn't you shirking hard work. It's helping you to keep your head up and **remain motivated**.

Quite often, they won't need to have the answers because you'll find them yourself through talking. And you can ask them about non-school stuff too! Worried about something you've seen on social media? Fallen out with a friend? Tell someone if things are bothering you. These things still happen, even in exam season, and **having a mentor will help you get through them, so you can focus on the stuff that really matters**.

GET YOUR DOPAMINE BOOST

Dopamine is the happy hormone and you can get it from just being around the people you love! Whether it's spending timing with a close friend, getting a cuddle from a parent or a fist bump from your big brother and a chat about how his online gaming is going, it's a dose of normal life with those people who are there for you every day. It helps remind you that the world's still turning and other things are happening – use them to have a whinge, a cry, a moan or a **laugh** . . . then get back on with what you're doing. This will make you happy, improve your wellbeing and supercharge your motivation.

MONITOR YOUR IMPACT

As you chip away at your revision, day after day, you will start to see the impact. Being able to confidently answer a question on something you couldn't do a couple of weeks ago, because of the graft you've put in, is a hugely **positive motivational tool**. It's great to know that what you're doing is working and that you're another step closer to achieving your goals!

CELEBRATE YOU!

Talking to yourself in the mirror and saying how proud you are of what you're doing can be great, even if it might feel a bit weird! Listing the things you've actually done can feel really satisfying too. Positive self-talk that involves celebrating **YOU** and **YOUR** achievements is scientifically linked to developing strategies to cope with emotional stress and anxiety. **Focus on the stuff you are doing and you'll feel so much more motivated to continue.**

PRESS RESET

There are very occasional days or moments where you simply need to press the **reset button** and step back for a bit. Repeated stressful moments release more and more stress hormones into your body, and **there are times when you just need to take a break**.

But don't press the button too often — you don't want it to become your only response to things that are hard (because plenty is going to be), but using it sparingly, when it's needed, **is only human**.

One great way of taking a break **AND** getting motivated and improving your focus is to **do sport**. Doing exercise for at least thirty minutes a day is linked with improved brain function and overall health. Physical activity floods your brain with neurotransmitters such as dopamine and serotonin, decreasing anxiety and increasing focus.

SO GET OUT THERE FOR A WALK, RUN OR GYM SESSION – IT'LL DO WONDERS FOR FEEDING THAT MOTIVATION MONSTER!

COUNT DOWN THE DAYS

A really great motivational tool is to create a countdown to your exams. Mark up the days on your calendar and literally say out loud '25 days to go' . . . '10 days to go' as you cross off the days. Nothing motivates the mind like knowing exactly how long you have left to go.

VISUALISE SUCCESS

Visualisation is a technique you can use to create a strong mental image of your goals. There are many different ways to do it, and they all help with motivation. You can:

- **MENTALLY REHEARSE:** This is when you walk yourself through each task you need to complete before you do it and envision the success you're going to have in the future. This technique increases resilience and focus. For example: Imagine you're walking into that exam, fully prepared, feeling confident. You sit down and you're in the zone, answering question after question. You walk out, and then months later, you open that letter – you aced it!! You feel relief, happiness and pride.
- **MAKE A VISION BOARD:** Use an online vision board or a sketchbook to pull together images of your

success and the future life you want, and use it to motivate you when times get tough.

- **WRITE A DAILY JOURNAL:** It helps to review the things you've achieved and what you've managed to do well that day, and it will motivate you to continue tomorrow.

It's true to say that when you're faced with your results in a few months' time, you won't need any motivation to tear open the envelope and find out how things have gone. But your success won't be because of how quickly you tore open the envelope - it will be because of the **homework**, the **after-school classes**, going out for some **fresh air** and a walk when things weren't working quite so well and the **positive attitude** you had throughout the busy exam season. Keeping yourself **motivated** to manage your exam schedule and **not getting crushed by it feeling absolutely relentless is tough**, but you can do it!

BE A MOTIVATION MONSTER
AND ROAR!

55

7

SPRING-CLEAN YOUR STUDIES

No matter where you are in your revision journey, it's always helpful to know whether your routines are in place, your revision plan is working and you're hitting the heights of doing your best . . . or just about getting by.

This is where we just need to step in and spring-clean our studies. **Get your feather duster ready!**

RETURN TO YOUR NOTES

Start from the beginning and look over your notes.

- Do they make sense?
- Do they need rewriting?
- Are they complete nonsense and you can't believe what you wrote?

Rewrite the ones that don't work for you — by doing this, you're drawing that knowledge back from your long-term memory. *(For more on how your brain stores memories, and how you can hack it, go to page 87.)*

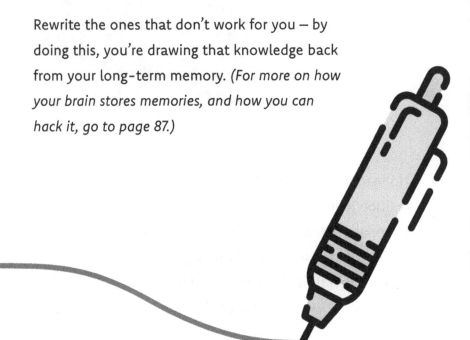

LOOK AT YOUR TOPIC LISTS

At the beginning of your course, your teachers in all your lessons will likely have given you a sheet which tells you what you will learn, when and where in the course. With a set of red, amber and green felt-tip pens, go through that list of topics, one by one, and give yourself a rating:

Red: There's loads of work to do, and I'm definitely not confident.

Amber: Meh, this is fine. I'm doing OK, and I can remember it (more or less).

Green: Nailed it. Bosh. Done. Thanks for coming – see you later.

Now you know the subjects you feel confident in and the areas where you really need to focus.

LOOK AT WHAT'S TO COME

Have a look at where you need to be going and what you'll be learning next. Even though it might seem overwhelming, knowing what's in front of you is the first step towards getting it done. It will enable you to focus on the things that really matter and start your revision with a bang.

Once all that's done, then you should have something that is underrated by everyone, of every age, in every walk of life: **clarity.**

Like the beautiful moment when the water falls out of your ear after you've been swimming, and you don't have to worry about it sloshing about inside your brain any more, feeling that things are clear is a nice feeling.

STEP INTO YOUR
STUDIES WITH A
REALLY CLEAR IDEA
OF YOUR GOALS,
WHERE YOU ARE IN
RELATION TO THEM
RIGHT NOW AND WHAT
YOU'RE GOING TO DO
NEXT. THAT, MY FRIEND,
IS A PLAN.

8

OVERCOME OBSTACLES

I'd love to be able to tell you that nothing's going to go wrong across your **exam** period, but I'm afraid there are likely to be some serious **obstacles** to climbing that mountain of study that is looming in front of you. They might be:

- Worry, stress and panic
- Illness
- Family and friendship problems
- School problems

Whatever the issue getting in your way, the main thing to remember is that **there is action you can take**, because you are in charge. **So, grab your ropes and gear, put on those grippy hiking boots and get ready to crush whatever's in your way!**

REFRAME THAT BRAIN

OK, it might feel like the world is against you and there is no possible way you can cram enough study into your brain to succeed in your exams. Even the foothills of that study mountain are too steep.

When you face obstacles, try **cognitive reframing**. It might sound like a fancy scientific term, but all it means is that you should try looking at a situation from a different perspective.

BUT HOW?

Whenever you face a problem that feels overwhelming, try **zooming out** and taking a **broader perspective**. For example:

ZOOMED IN: You're unwell and all you can think of is how you're missing valuable revision time being all snotty and gross, and *if I don't revise soon I'm going to fail EVERYTHING and my life WILL BE RUINED!*

ZOOMED OUT: Take a breath. Zoom out. Ask yourself these questions: *Is that realistic? Will I really ruin everything by taking time to recover for a few days? What is the evidence behind that thought? What does the bigger picture look like?*

ZOOMED IN: You're having trouble at school — you can't seem to do ANYTHING right, whether it's homework or lessons or even making time to see your friends. *What is wrong with me?*

ZOOMED OUT: Reframe that brain. *Am I misinterpreting the situation? Is there really nothing I am doing right? Do facts really support this, or am I thinking this out of habit?*

Asking yourself honest questions about your problems helps **reframe your brain** and can put you into a more positive mindset, which, as we know, is proven to make a big difference to your ability to learn and revise.

YOU CAN ALSO TRY WRITING YOUR PROBLEMS LIKE THIS:

Problem	Advice	How to help yourself
Minor bump in the road: *Practice exams are going badly*	*Ask friends if they can help. If not, turn to teachers for guidance or family for support*	*Reflect on the situation and the impact it's having. Accept it and make a plan to deal with the situation*
Giant obstacle in the road: *Parents are getting divorced* *You broke your arm during exam preparation*	*Some things are so big they're out of your control.* *It's definitely time for school and family to step in and help*	*Be as open and honest as you can with school* *Find out what support is available to you*

This is a tough time in your life – nobody doubts that one little bit – so when things are difficult and life is a little rough, take a bit of weight off and give yourself a break. Exams assess how sophisticated your knowledge about your subjects is, of course, but they are also to see how good you are at dealing with the pressure. They're not designed that way, but to perform well for that sustained period of time takes **guts, determination, discipline and heart**.

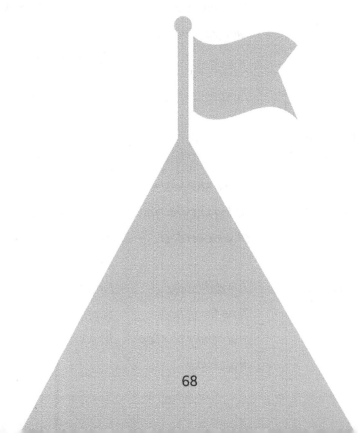

IT'S GOING TO BE FINE.
ASSESS WHAT IS GOING
ON, REFRAME THAT
BRAIN BY ZOOMING
OUT, AND YOU'LL
CRUSH THOSE
OBSTACLES IN
NO TIME.

PART TWO

ACE
REVISION

If I said to you that revision is superbly glamorous, glorious and will always feel amazing to do, I'd be lying. Revision isn't any of those things, but it is important.

When it's done right, it is something you can work at, train at and improve over time. It also does not need to be done for hour, after hour, after hour, after hour. Get it right, and it should be done in blocks, little and often, with regular breaks and plenty of time for you to do some stuff you want to do.

So, let's dive in and see why we do it, some ways you can do it and how it's going to help you get ready and set for those exams . . .

9

TRUSTED TECHNIQUES

Revision works with three main principles in mind:

- **Forgetting**
- **Remembering**
- **Practising**

The first time you cover a particular topic, it'll very likely be in one of your lessons, and you'll probably forget it not long after. Revision is all about remembering it and practising again and again so it is firmly stuck in that brain of yours for when you need it most.

Try these trusted methods:

BLURTING

Blurting is exactly what you're thinking about when you hear the word — it's all about 'blurting' out information uncontrollably. It's a good starting point that helps you identify what you know and what needs further work.

Try this: Grab a pen and paper and whichever notes you want to revise. Read a section of those notes, set a five-minute timer . . . and . . . wait for it . . . **BLURT.**

Write down everything you can remember about that topic in the time you have. Dates, formulae, important characters — whatever it is you can think of. Afterwards, compare that to your textbook or notes. See what you managed to recall and what needs more study.

Blurting makes your brain work hard and, by doing it again and again, sets down crucial information in your long-term memory.

FLASH CARDS

Flash cards are small note cards with important information on them, which can be in bullet-point, note or diagram form. The act of writing up notes on them is helpful for remembering, but so is using them as revision aids once that's done.

If the past tense of 'hablar' in Spanish is defeating you, then copy out how it conjugates on to a flash card and read it out loud. Then turn the card over and try to remember what was on it. You'll get some of it right; you'll get some of it wrong. But eventually, 'recordarás' (that means 'you will remember' in Spanish!) the whole lot in one go!

This technique uses **active recall** – forcing your brain to get into gear and do the really hard work of dredging a bit of information up from deep within!

You can also stick flash cards up on your bedroom wall, in the kitchen or even in the bathroom! That way, when you're going about your day, you can sneak in a moment or two of revision.

MIND MAPS

If you're revising the marketing process in business studies, it's super easy to remember 'the four Ps': **product, place, price and promotion**. However, remembering just those four things won't impress those examiners all that much.

Put each one of them into a mind map. Place 'product' in the middle of a piece of paper and draw branches coming off it, adding more information relating to it, such as 'customers', 'manufacturing' and 'cost'.

The act of creating the mind map is fun, makes complex ideas easier to understand, will show yourself the depth of your knowledge on a topic and can aid memory recall.

DUAL CODING

Closely linked to mind maps is the concept of dual coding. This is where you **combine words and visuals for even more effective revision**.

Mind maps, infographics, timelines, diagrams, drawings and even little comic strips — these are all ways of turning big chunks of text into visuals that your brain will find easier to recall.

For example: Try putting the key dates of your Second World War history module into a timeline poster you can stick up on your wall, like this:

JANUARY 1933:

Hitler becomes Chancellor of Germany

MARCH 1938:

German 'Anschluss' with Austria

MARCH 1939:

Hitler invades Czechoslovakia

SEPTEMBER 1939:

Britain and France declare war

You could also draw your own **diagram of a cell** with important information around it, create a **comic strip** featuring important figures in *Macbeth* or use an **online infographic creator** to create a visual representation of the formula and important information you've been learning in chemistry.

Studies show that students who revise using a combination of words and visuals have better recall compared to those who revise purely with words. **Give it a try!**

If you think of revision as a **continuous cycle which sits alongside schoolwork, homework and everything else** you have to do, it'll become one of those habits that we know are so, so important. Start with ten minutes per day, build up to twenty minutes when you're focusing for assessments, and then work up to a maximum of three hours per day in those periods around the final exams.

Revision should be repeated, regular, reasonable, robust, and what's more:

I CAN GIVE MY CAST-IRON, 100%, MR BURTON GUARANTEE THAT IF YOU DO THESE THINGS AND USE THESE TRUSTED TECHNIQUES, YOU WILL MAKE REVISION MUCH MORE USEFUL AND BENEFICIAL – AND MUCH LESS BORING AND BOTHERSOME.

10

CREATIVE
COLOUR-CODING

Revision strategies will get you to the point where you're actively learning the stuff you need to, but it's important to know how to make **useful** and **solid notes**, and then how to get the most out of them. Oh, and why not make them colourful?

NOTES, BULLET POINTS AND REVISION POINTS

Whatever you call them, they need to be **good**. The trick to ending up with good notes that don't leave you thinking, *'Eh? What does that mean?'* is making sure you identify the important stuff you need to revise.

Let's take a classic example from science – **sound waves.** You won't need to remember every single word your teacher said or know every single word you wrote down in your notes. What matters is the key information. For instance, you might have a list of facts, such as:

- Sound travels in waves
- Sound is created by vibrations in the waves
- We hear by waves going into the human ear
- The waves make the eardrum vibrate
- Bones send the vibrations to the cochlea
- The cochlea sends electrical messages to the brain through the cochlear nerve

These bullet points are fine, but have you noticed that each pair is saying **similar things?** If you pick out the **keywords** – the ones that are crucially and critically important – you would be able to get combine them and get them down to three rather than six.

For example:

- Sound is created by vibrations and travels as a wave
- Waves make the eardrum vibrate, allowing us to hear
- The vibrations in the ear travel to the cochlea, which then go to the brain through the cochlear nerve

Have a go with your revision points – how can you pare them down so that you're including the **key points** in the most **concise** way? And how can you colour-code them so that you're getting the information you need at a glance?

Perhaps anything on a pink sticky note stands for science and anything on a blue sticky note is for English?

Picking colours for different topics is a great way to practise dual coding and combine visual and text-based learning. It also prompts the more creative part of your brain to sit up and take note (quite literally!).

RED, AMBER OR GREEN – 'RAGGING'

Because your revision schedule is going to be a marathon, not a sprint, you are going to go back to your notes and your lists lots of times. Being clear about what you know and what you don't know is key.

Make a list of a few topics within your subject areas that you're not quite sure about. For example:

PHYSICS

- Forces
- Electric circuits
- Material density

ENGLISH LITERATURE

- *A Christmas Carol*
- Unseen poetry
- *Macbeth*

Within each of these, there are loads of mini-topics and bits of information you need to feel confident about.

A helpful thing to do is to mark them as **red, green** or **amber**, or **'RAG'** them.

RED = areas you're not really confident about
AMBER = areas you can manage but where you could do with more practice
GREEN = areas you know off by heart and are comfortable and confident with

For example, if you were going to **RAG** your knowledge of forces, your list might look like this:

PHYSICS: FORCES

- Scalars and vectors – **YELLOW**
- Speed and velocity – **GREEN**
- Distance and velocity/time graphs – **YELLOW**
- Acceleration and deceleration – **GREEN**
- Calculating acceleration – **RED**
- Measuring speed – **YELLOW**

You can **use highlighters** or different **coloured pens** to make each point super obvious, or simply mark up the status next to each topic. Either way, your brain will quickly get the hint about which topics you need to focus on more.

HIGHLIGHT

You can do something similar when you are **highlighting important areas in your notes.** Instead of covering them in a sea of bright yellow marker, why not use **yellow** for key dates, **pink** for important formulae and **green** for critical information?

USE COLOUR EFFECTIVELY AND IT WILL FLICK THAT SWITCH IN YOUR BRAIN THAT SAYS, 'REMEMBER THIS, IT'S IMPORTANT!'

11

HACK YOUR BRAIN

The human brain is an **amazing thing**. It lets you smell, taste, touch, see and hear. It never switches off and it doesn't need to be taken into a shop when it breaks down, for a technician to say, *'Errrm, just give it a whack and it'll be all right!'*

Without doubt, your brain is going to help you in your exams. However, you need to help your brain too. In fact, **you need to HACK IT!** Don't worry, it won't hurt. Hacking it will give you **much more room to store the information you need to pass your exams.**

That means the brain's memory needs to be organised – and **it is!** It has different areas which are responsible for different functions. Here are some of them:

The **amygdala** is the bit of your brain that regulates emotions

The **cerebellum** co-ordinates movement and balance

The **prefrontal cortex** helps with planning and decision-making

The **hippocampus** is involved in long-term memory formation and retrieval

SO WHAT?

If you want to use your memories, all of the various parts of the brain need to **work together to help you**. On the next few pages are some strategies you can use to help recall information. Why not give each one a go and see which helps you to turn information from your lessons into memories and then into marks in your exams?

CHUNKING

A great way of remembering is to chunk together bits of relevant information. There are two different types: **pattern chunking** and **category chunking.**

Pattern chunking involves remembering patterns as chunks of information. When you need to remember your mum's mobile number to write it into your friend's phone when your battery dies, you might not recall all eleven numbers in one go. But maybe you can remember it if you break it down into two chunks of five and six digits:
01234 567890

The same goes if you want to remember the first ten digits of pi. You could break it down into five chunks of two:
3.1   41   59   26   53

Category chunking stops you from getting cognitive overload. If you need to remember parts of the human body for a science exam, for example, remembering every single part would be pretty much impossible. But if you group them into category chunks, such as **respiratory system, nervous system** and **muscular system,** then the information will be easier to recall. For example:

Respiratory system: nose, throat, trachea, lungs

Nervous system: brain, spinal cord, nerve network

Muscular system: oesophagus, stomach, small intestine, large intestine, anus

Or you could try it with the families and their affiliates in *Romeo and Juliet:*

Montagues: Romeo, Mercutio, Benvolio, Lady and Lord Montague

Capulets: Juliet, Tybalt, Lord and Lady Capulet, Nurse

MNEMONICS

Mnemonics are named after the Greek goddess of memory, Mnemosyne. They are helpful devices involving patterns of letters that aid memory recall. The most famous one is probably **ROY G BIV**. No, not an unusually named substitute teacher, but the colours of the rainbow: **red, orange, yellow, green, blue, indigo, violet.**

Mnemonics don't just have to be letters, though – they can also be **made-up phrases.** For example, if you need to remember the features of a river for a geography exam, try

'So Many Tigers Can Make Fighting Dangerous'.

The initial letters will help you recall:

Source
Mouth
Tributaries
Channel
Meanders
Floodplains
Deltas

MEMORY PALACE

Memory palaces are places where you can store information for easy recall – they are vast structures full of information just waiting for you to grab! But wait, I know what you're thinking. You can't take a whole palace into the exam hall with you. Well, you can – if it's inside your mind!

To create your very own palace, choose somewhere you know well. This example uses your home, but it could be your school or even somewhere outside, like the route to your gran's.

Now make a list of things you want to remember – let's say, key moments in *Macbeth*.

Take one moment, such as Macbeth's first meeting with the three witches. Close your eyes and plonk them right in the middle of your living room. Give it loads of atmosphere and really feel the witches there, hanging out on your mum's favourite rug, making all sorts of mess with their potions.

Then go into the kitchen and find Lady Macbeth furiously scrubbing her hands in the sink, desperately trying to get that 'damned spot' of blood off her hands.

Continue round the house, adding moments here and there, until you've deposited things you need to remember all the way round your house. Mentally revisit your memory palace regularly, so that you keep those important moments, dates, facts or figures fresh in your mind and ready to use.

SINGING

It might sound daft, but if you're musically inclined, **singing your revision can help**. Replace the words of your favourite songs with key information you want to remember and you'll be amazed at how quickly 'Shake It Off' becomes a way of remembering the marketing process for your business studies exam. One word of warning, though: you'll be singing your own words forever more!

Whether you use these tips or you've got your own, whatever technique you use will only work if you're organised about what you want to remember and if you give yourself time to do it. Your brain's set up to help you, so what's stopping you?

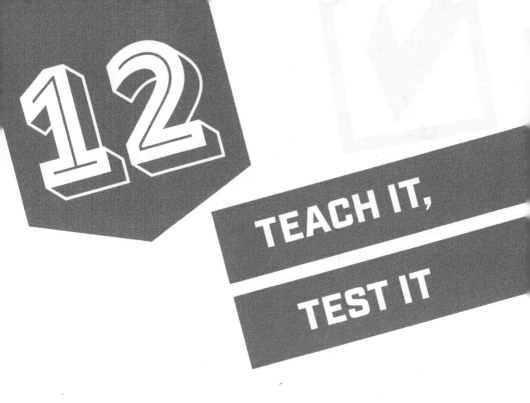

12

TEACH IT, TEST IT

You might be forgiven for thinking that during exam season, it's all about revision, revision, revision. (Well, OK, it is.) BUT — **it can also be about teaching,** too. Teaching someone else is a super effective way of helping you understand a topic inside out.

To teach well, you have to organise your thoughts, work out how you're going to explain your topic and present the information in as clear a way as possible. Which is just what you need to do in your exams!

 TEACH IT

Pick a topic you're currently feeling a bit unsure of. Then find a willing student. It could be a parent, sibling or other relative, or it could be your pet cat Pickles, or even that sad-looking house plant in the corner that you haven't watered for months.

Choose a time when you're going to teach them all about coastal erosion in the UK or the imperfect tense in Spanish, and then get to work.

STEP 1: KNOW YOUR TOPIC

Research your subject thoroughly and make sure you know your stuff.

STEP 2: PICK YOUR GOALS

What specifically do you want your student to know by the end of your lesson? Identify some key learning that you want them to take away with them.

STEP 3: PLAN LESSON

Plan how you are going to present the lesson. What important vocabulary or concepts will you need to explain? How are you going to keep things engaging?

STEP 4: PRESENT

Sit your student down and present your lesson. Throw in fun activities such as brainstorming, debates and quizzes to get them thinking. (This could be difficult with the house plant or Pickles, but you never know.)

STEP 5: REVIEW

Recap the lesson and test your student on what they know. Don't be tempted to skip this step. Reviewing what your student knows will tell you whether or not they've really understood. If they haven't, maybe you haven't understood the topic either!

Not only will organising your thoughts and teaching a lesson help you with your revision in the moment, it also will be much easier during your exams to remember that hilarious time you taught your mum quadratic equations or your dad the joys of covalent bonds!

STUDY GROUPS

You don't have to restrict your teaching to home. Why not gather a band of pals and form a study group? In study groups, you:

- Get the benefit of different ideas and perspectives on tough topics
- Boost your ability to remember information, because it's easier to remember a conversation you had about a subject than it is to remember reviewing notes
- Stay accountable to others – you can't slack off when your friends are depending on you
- Get feedback from trusted friends about what you need to work on

To form a study group, **just get together three to five people who want to work on a certain topic**. Pick a place to meet and bring your notes. You could have a plan for each session, where every person teaches a little bit about what they know, or you could make it really fun and design quizzes and games for each other.

Turn studying into the format of your favourite TV game show or separate yourself out into two teams and get competitive about who knows what. **Whatever you do, make sure you have a plan and focus on what you want to get out of each meeting.**

TEACH IT, TEST IT AND ACE THAT REVISION!

13

KNOW YOUR GAME PLAN

To ace your exams, you need a **game plan**. It might take some time to create, but it will save time in the long run. You want a plan that is:

- **SUSTAINABLE**

  It starts nice and early, gives you plenty to do, but not too much, and is based on revising more of the topics you're less sure about.

- **SAFE**

  It doesn't need you to get up at silly o'clock every morning and tie yourself to your desk from sunrise to sunset. It allows you time away for other things too.

- **SECURE**

  It leaves you feeling ready. As a result of the work you've done, you're ready and set to ace those exams!

TIMETABLE

Plan out the week ahead in detail. It might look something like this:

Time	Mon	Tues	Weds	Thurs	Fri	Sat	Sun
8 a.m.	Maths			English			Maths
9 a.m.	Maths			English			Maths
10 a.m.							
11 a.m.					Science		
12 p.m.			English		Science		
1 p.m.		Science	English		Science		
2 p.m.		Science			Science		
3 p.m.		Science			Science		
4 p.m.							
5 p.m.				English		English	
6 p.m.				English		English	

SCHEDULE

Then, at the start of each revision day, schedule a morning's worth of work, remembering the three Rs: **revise, rest, reward.**

For example:
8 a.m. – 8.30 a.m.: **BREAKFAST**

8.30 a.m. – 9 a.m.: **REVISE:** English literature

9 a.m. – 10 a.m.: **REST**

9.30 a.m. – 10 a.m.: **REVISE:** Physics

10.30 a.m. – 11 a.m.: **REST**

11 a.m. – 11.30 a.m.: **REVISE:** English literature

11.30 a.m. – 12 p.m.: **REVISE:** Maths

12 p.m. – 12.30 p.m.: **LUNCH**

12.30 p.m. – 1 p.m.: **REWARD:** Chat with a friend or play a video game for half an hour

Remember: go back to those subjects you're feeling more 'red' than 'green' about. Jot down your topics and think of each block of revision as thirty minutes split roughly in half: fifteen minutes revising and fifteen minutes practising.

What would you do differently from the example? You might think you'd like to spend longer on particular subjects — maybe an hour at a time — and cover a couple of topics. The choice is absolutely yours.

One really important thing to remember about your game plan is that it needs to be followed. It needs to be baked into your routine and become a habit. Try planning your routine out like the example — include evenings and weekends too.

1, 2, 3, 7

If you want to remember something tricky you've learnt, the 1, 2, 3, 7 technique can be a great one to build into your game plan. It works on the principle that a massive part of remembering something in the long term is forgetting it in the short term. So, to get something into our long-term memories, we take a clever approach to revisiting it regularly. It works like this:

DAY ONE: Take the information you want to remember, like the dates of key First World War battles, and make a revision card with bullet points.

DAY TWO: Rewrite the card from memory, checking what you got right and what you got wrong.

DAY THREE: Do the same again the next day. You are consolidating your revision.

DAY SEVEN: Leave it for four days, until day seven. Rewrite the card from memory again, and see how you've done.

7, 5, 3, 2

If the 1, 2, 3, 7 method works for you and you're not sick of numbers just yet, it's worth looking at the 7, 5, 3, 2 method as well. Rather than moving forward, this technique involves counting back from your exam, so it works well during exam season. Start on your exam day (day zero) and work backwards to build in slots to revise key topics on days two, three, five and seven.

SEVEN DAYS BEFORE EXAM: Make sure you have the key topics you need written out on to flash cards or organised in your notes folder.

FIVE DAYS BEFORE EXAM: Pinpoint some key revision techniques you're going to use and devote a study session to the exam in question.

THREE DAYS BEFORE EXAM: Test yourself on what you revised with five days to go. Tweak your revision and try again if it's not sticking.

TWO DAYS BEFORE EXAM: Test yourself a final time, and filling in any gaps in your knowledge.

DAY ZERO: Exam day!

80/20

This one isn't a technique, but it is something you can keep in mind when you develop your game plan: the 80/20 rule. It's used in all different walks of life, but when it comes to your revision, it means that: 80% of results – in this case your exam results – come from 20% of core material studied in your revision.

It's NOT about ignoring detail or skimming your notes; it's about working out what the **CORE knowledge** is that's going to give you the bulk of your marks.

Whatever you choose, there's lots out there that can help you with your game plan, but the only person who can decide to do it is – yes, you guessed it **– you!**

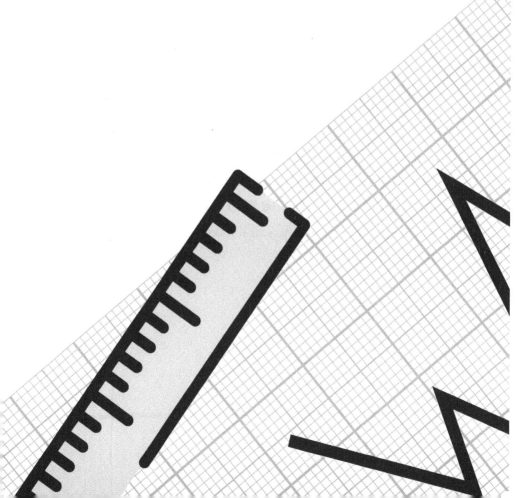

14

SMASH MOCKS AND PAST PAPERS

Mock exams are designed to help you feel comfortable with the real thing.

By taking them seriously, you'll have a really good chance to:

- Practise preparing properly
- Revise right
- Deal with study discipline
- Experience exam stress safely

Mock exams and practice papers give you **experience of what the real exams will look and feel like,** and how questions can be phrased. And, what's more, it's been scientifically proven that you retain more information if you test yourself than if you don't. So why wait for the real thing? Smash some mocks and practice tests now!

PLAN OF ATTACK

FIND OUT WHEN PRACTICE EXAMS ARE ON

School should tell you in really good time — make sure they're marked clearly on your calendar and be prepared to treat them seriously. This is a great opportunity to test what you know.

FIND PAST PAPERS

Past papers are available on exam boards' websites — if you can't find them, ask your teachers where to look.

ORGANISE THE TOPICS THAT NEED REVISING

Use the red/amber/green method to prioritise what you need to know beforehand.

WORK OUT WHICH TECHNIQUES YOU'RE GOING TO USE

Are you going for the 1, 2, 3, 7 method, mind mapping or flash cards? Is this your chance to BLURT everything, or maybe teach someone you know? Now is your chance to try out the different methods and see which ones work for you.

CRUNCH TIME

If you're doing mocks, **treat them seriously.** They're an **amazing chance to gain confidence** in what you're doing, find out how you're performing right now and get estimated grades that could be really useful to show colleges or potential apprenticeships how you might do.

It's also great to get validation for all the **hard work** you're putting in. Behavioural science shows that humans don't necessarily always need to have 'stuff' (presents or similar) to let us know we've done well.

WE REACT MORE POSITIVELY WHEN GET FEEDBACK FROM PEOPLE LIKE TEACHERS OR OUR FAMILY.

Past papers are perfect for testing yourself in your own time. You can also find the mark schemes on the exam boards' websites, as well as the 'model answers', so it's the perfect way to check **EXACTLY** what examiners are looking for, AND to review which revision techniques work for you and where you are falling short.

IF YOU TAKE MOCKS AND PAST PAPERS SERIOUSLY, THEY CAN BE AN ABSOLUTELY KEY PART OF ACING YOUR EXAMS.

15
TAKE
TIME OUT

It might not be something you expected to read in this book, **but taking time out to rest is super important** to your studies. It's a big part of making sure your revision is sustainable, safe and secure.

You can't sustain any level of performance if you don't **take a break**. You're not being safe with your mental or physical health if you're cramming for sixteen hours a day, and your confidence will not be secure if you are so worried that you end up doing far too much.

A successful plan builds in breaks, rests and time to chill. Doing what you enjoy releases happy hormones in your brain, which in turn helps you to become more relaxed and puts you in a better headspace.

Doing too much can lead to burnout. This comes from overworking and ignoring your wellbeing in pursuit of more and more and more revision.

BURNOUT LOOKS LIKE THIS:

- **IRRITABILITY:** Getting annoyed all the time and snapping at people

- **FRUSTRATION:** Feeling as if what you're doing isn't enough and isn't helping

- **LACK OF MOTIVATION:** Forgetting your goals or feeling like you want to give up on them

- **TIREDNESS:** Feeling physically exhausted because of the work you've done

- **INSOMNIA:** Being unable to switch off and go to sleep

- **BRAIN FOG:** Your thoughts feeling all over the place and not seeming to make sense

If it's got to the point where you are burnt out, then it's vital that you get your trusted adults to take you to the GP and get some help. Also speak to school — they have people who can, want to and will help.

But to avoid burnout becoming a problem, there are simple steps you can take. You can do it, but you have to trust that taking time away from revision sometimes is not a bad thing. Quite the opposite, in fact: it's vital.

EXERCISE

Walk, run, jog, hike, limbo dance, kick a football, smash a cricket ball. It doesn't matter what, but it matters that it happens. Physical exercise is proven to reduce stress hormones and boost endorphins — taking down the negatives and pumping up the positive vibes in your body and mind.

GET OUTSIDE

Even if it's fresh air on the front step, getting your head away from the laptop or revision is key. Getting outside is proven to boost immunity, and doing activities outside can even reduce symptoms of anxiety and depression. It also helps with sleep, which is crucial to feeling good.

MAKE TIME FOR SOCIALISING

Sharing worries and problems with your friends, who are going through the same thing, will often shift your mindset away from things being a problem, to focusing on the solutions instead. It's also key to your exam success to put them into context: even in exam mode, you need to remember that you are still a human being, with friends, emotions and people you care for.

HYDRATION

Keeping a constant flow of water is vital for keeping you healthy. Studies have shown that drinking water can increase blood flow to that pink thing in your skull, prevents headaches and can even prevent eye strain.

SELF-CARE

Whether it's a bath, an early night with a soppy film in bed or painting your toenails in all the colours of the rainbow, taking time for you — just you — to breathe and reflect on things will do your body and mind the world of good. Chilling out and relaxing doesn't happen by accident, though; you can still plan for it. So download the film before you start revising in the afternoon, make sure your dad hasn't used all the hot water for his bath . . . and you'll have something special to look forward to as a treat for yourself.

POSITIVE AFFIRMATIONS

Sometimes it can be easy to forget that stuff in the heat of a busy revision schedule with exam after exam on a repetitive loop. Take time to tell yourself, firmly, in a mirror, positive things about yourself, your worth and your qualities . . . and believe it.

I am doing enough.
I am doing my best.
I am a good person and deserve to be happy.

Affirmations replace negative thoughts with positive ones, actively rewiring the way your brain works and encouraging positive mood.

MEDITATION

Meditation is amazing at relaxing you and distracting you from the busyness of your mind, and it has been used for millennia across lots of different cultures. It has been shown to deactivate the amygdala, which is associated with fear, and activate the prefrontal cortex, which is associated with happiness.

Try this simple meditation to help clear your mind and prepare yourself for studying:

Step 1: Find a quiet spot and make yourself comfortable.

Step 2: Close your eyes and focus on your breathing, in and out, in and out.

Step 3: Stay focused on your breathing. Notice when your mind begins to wander off, and pull it back to that in and out sensation of your breath.

Step 4: After ten minutes, or when you feel it's time to stop, bring your meditation to a close and open your eyes again.

Result: Noticing when your mind wanders off is part of mindfulness, which makes you more aware of what's going on in the present moment. It helps to focus you, and settle your mind.

IF YOU CRAM YOUR REVISION, YOU'LL FEEL COMPLETELY OVERWHELMED AND NOT GET THE BENEFIT FROM IT. TAKE YOUR TIME. TAKE TIME OUT. GO AGAIN.

16

JUST BREATHE

It's natural to worry, and it's very normal for that worry to affect how you feel. It's quite likely that, at this point in your life, you've never been through as much pressure as you're going through now that your exams loom into view. That's why it's important to breathe.

**Breathe in. Breathe out.
Breathe in. Breathe out.**

Why am I telling you to breathe? 'It's an involuntary function of the autonomic nervous system, you moron,' I hear you say. Well, it's simple. I want you to focus on it.

Controlled breathing and breathwork include a variety of different breathing techniques that do loads to reduce stress. They lower your heart rate, get more oxygen into your blood (which might be lacking when you feel panicked and overwhelmed), and can leave you feeling calmer pretty much instantly.

There are loads of techniques you can use to handle the myriad challenges assaulting you from all sides, and looking online will lead you to a million and one of them. I'm sure you'll find one that works for you, but here are a few popular ones to try.

BOX BREATHING

Box breathing — also known as four-square breathing — is a simple technique that is used in all walks of life, including in the police and army, to deal with stressful moments. It goes like this:

Step 1: Breathe in deeply, counting to four.

Step 4: Hold for four seconds, then repeat until you start to feel calmer.

Step 2: Hold that deep breath for four seconds.

Step 3: Breathe out through your mouth for four seconds.

Visualising a box, like the one above, helps you keep your breathing on track and gives the method its name. It helps you cope with panic and stress, and stay calm when things start to become overwhelming.

LION'S BREATH

No, don't worry, you don't have to go to the zoo, and please don't put your face anywhere near a lion's. YOU are the one with the lion breath. At least according to this method.

Step 1: Get comfortable in a seated position.

Step 2: Inhale deeply through your nose, keeping your eyes wide open.

Step 3: Open your eyes wide and stick out your tongue.

Step 4: When you exhale, made a loud 'haaa' sound, a bit like a lion's roar.

Step 5: Repeat two to three times.

This breathing technique is perfect for relieving tension in your face and chest, leaving you feeling fierce!

EQUAL BREATHING

This technique focuses on making your inhalations and exhalations equal — well, it was in the name after all!

Simply get comfortable, then choose a breathing count that works for you. Between three and five is usually best. Then, maintain equal inhales and exhales of that number. It can reduce blood pressure and increase oxygen to the brain, and it can be done almost anywhere.

BEE BREATHING

Ever wanted to breathe like a bee? Well, that's not quite what this is about, but the bee-breathing method is proven to have an instant calming and soothing effect.

Step 1: Get comfortable in a seated position.

Step 2: Close your eyes and let the muscles in your face relax.

Step 3: Place your fingers on the little bit of cartilage at the entrance to your ears.

Step 4: Gently inhale, pressing your fingers more firmly into the side of your ears.

Step 5: With your mouth closed, make a gentle humming noise – like a bee!

Keep going for as long as is comfortable.

Whichever technique you try, it's good to know that the power of breathing can reduce stress and anxiety, and that these methods are there for you whenever you need them.

17

CRUSH THE CURVE

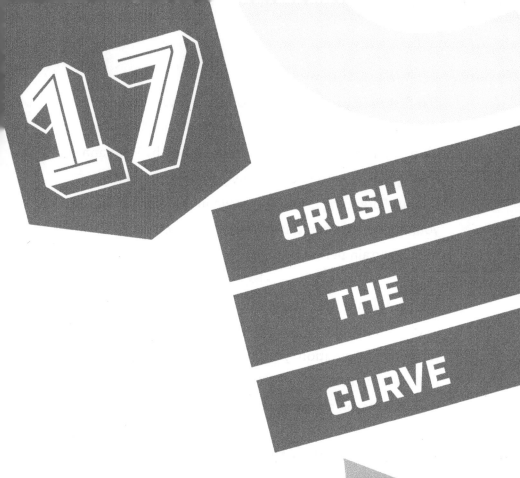

If you go back a few chapters, you'll remember we were talking about how your **brain stores information**. (Perhaps you've forgotten already, which is ironic!) If you want to crush your revision, you have to keep revisiting the things you've learnt, so that they are locked down as consolidated memories in your brain.

The first time you are taught something, you usually only retain a tiny portion of it over the following week. It's a phenomenon that was first described by Hermann Ebbinghaus, a ninteenth century psychologist, in his famous Forgetting Curve. As shown in the graph opposite, your ability to retain things you've learnt drops off steeply after a certain period of time.

After you leave your lessons, for example, you remember loads. But just a day later, if you don't force yourself to recall the information, you'll only remember about 40% of it. A week later, only 20%. A month later. . . err, what was that lesson about again?

The way to stop forgetting is to recall key information, time after time. The more times you do it, the more you remember. Going back to the information and learning it, again and again, will make sure you overcome the dreaded curve of forgetfulness. That way, you won't end up in an exam with a puzzled expression on your face, desperately chewing the end of your pencil in panic.

THE FORGETTING CURVE

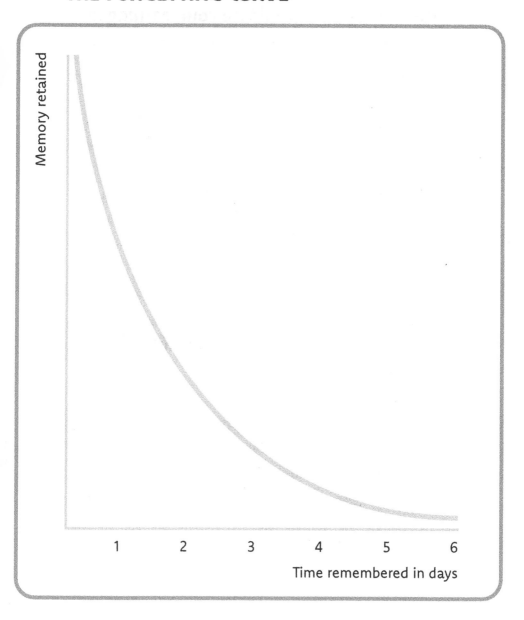

Teachers recapping things throughout the year helps you consolidate your learning in this way. But you can do it too, making it a key part of revision as you approach your exams.

INTERLEAVING

A technique called interleaving is designed to strengthen topic knowledge by spacing out chunks of revision in short bursts. Each chunk can then be revisited over a few days or weeks, rather than it being crammed in all at once. Returning to knowledge you've previously learnt will help to consolidate it in your brain.

Go back to your revision plans, think about all that we've looked at here, **and ask yourself these questions:**

- Have you given yourself enough chances to recall knowledge and consolidate it?
- Have you spaced topics out enough so that you're not just repeating something you've literally only just covered five minutes ago?
- Are there any topics you think you need to go back to which are really important foundations for the rest of

your knowledge? For example, key dates in history or key plot points from plays.

- Can you confidently list the key bits of knowledge you need for the main topics in your subjects?

Then find an example of a topic you marked as red when you did your red, amber, green ratings. With the information from the previous page in mind, plan to revise that topic and revisit it after twenty-four hours, after a week, after two weeks and then after a month. Every time you go back to it, you'll need to stretch your brain a little less to find that memory.

There's nothing wrong with going back to your plan and changing it so it does a better job for you. Remember, examiners aren't going to give anyone a single point on any exam paper for their revision schedule being beautifully presented. What they will be looking for is the impact of those plans on your wide and deep understanding of the subject.

Revisiting topics is part of the curve of remembering — and you shouldn't forget that. Remind me: what was I talking about again?

18

VANQUISH PROCRASTINATION

Inside your brain there is a fight going on. It's between the prefrontal cortex, which is responsible for planning, and the limbic system, where pleasure is generated. **The limbic system wants you to get away from revision,** because, let's face it, it's not always the most pleasurable thing in the world, whereas the prefrontal cortex knows you need to hunker down and get things done.

If the limbic system wins, that's when you get up to make a cup of tea, organise your pens, tidy your bedroom or simply do anything to avoid what you know you should be doing. You've grabbed that short-term reward in favour of long-term success.

It takes a lot, but there are ways to vanquish the beast of procrastination — and help your prefrontal cortex come out on top.

BEING MINDFUL

Mindfulness is simply the state of being aware of something going on in the present moment and accepting/noticing the feelings and thoughts that are occurring. Practising it can be super helpful for noticing your bad procrastination habits.

Think back to the chapter about habit formation. There are cues, cravings, responses and rewards involved with bad habits as well as good. Step back and think about the cues related to your procrastination. Is it when you see your phone and can't help but pick it up? Is it when you feel overwhelmed and just want to run away from what you're doing?

Noticing what is making you procrastinate can help you break the bad habit cycle and put new, good habits in place. Speaking of phones . . .

TURN IT OFF!

Phones are addictive. Receiving a notification gives our brains a tiny dopamine hit, which doesn't last long . . . and soon leaves our brains wanting another one. Dopamine is a chemical that's usually released when we do something fun — eating chocolate, riding rollercoasters or meeting friends — so getting trapped in a cycle of scrolling to make ourselves get that hit is not only a royal way of wasting time, but it's also a never-ending cycle which will never satisfy us.

Phones do have their advantages — revision resources, social connections with pals and that beautiful moment later in the summer when you can text your loved ones and tell them how amazingly well you've done. So, while we're not chucking them in the bin, we are going to limit the use of them. It helps if you:

TRACK YOUR USE AND SET A GOAL

You'll be shocked at the hours you spend on your phone. Track your screen time over a week and set a goal to reduce it by 10% in week one, another 10% in the following week, and so on.

CHARGE YOUR PHONE AWAY FROM YOU

Charge your devices across the room or even in a different room, so that you have to physically get up to get them — it will discourage you from scrolling on them all night in bed or at your desk when you're working.

PUT A RUBBER BAND AROUND THE SCREEN

This sounds crackers, but stay with me. You can easily answer your phone and you know who's calling you, but texting, social media and searching for pictures of monkeys in IKEA in parka jackets is much more difficult.

APP-LY SOME COMMON SENSE

There are apps you can download which can keep your mind in the game. They lock certain functions on your phone for you for a specific amount of time. Download one and set it up to help keep those eyes on the right stuff.

Other things that help us with procrastination are:

MAKING CONSEQUENCES IMMEDIATE

Putting your pen down and scrolling on your phone for a while is not going to cause you to do badly in your exams right now. That comes later. So it's easy to not worry about it too much.

Bring the consequences of your actions forward by building in some accountability. Plan a study session with a friend, so you can't get out of it. Tell a parent precisely what your revision plan is that day, so that they can ask you about it later.

KEEP A TIDY WORKSPACE

Keep your workspace tidy, clear of junk and fuss and mess, and all the other distractions that could give you an excuse to spend twenty-five minutes clearing up (again). It is vital that the place you're working is free from distractions, as much as possible. Remember that cognitive load stuff we talked about? The room you're in, how well organised your work is and how easy it is to concentrate all factor in to how much benefit your revision will have.

NATURAL LIGHT

Human beings need loads of natural light. It's something we've evolved to crave. Making sure you revise in a place that has a window can improve your wellbeing, reduce stress, headaches and eye strain, and can actually make you do more.

BLOCK OUT TIME IN YOUR DIARY

Revision is more likely to happen if you make time that is dedicated to it. Make it clear to yourself when that time is – so that you feel compelled to do it, so you're accountable for it and so it's something that is going to happen. If you use a shared family calendar, all the better – that way, everyone else can make sure you're getting on with things, too.

REWARDS

We've touched on rewards before. To make it clear, they should not be things that distract you – they should spur you on. I'm not suggesting booking yourself a fortnight-long Caribbean cruise for revising thirty minutes of homeostasis. But there's nothing wrong with putting a satisfying green tick next to your topic list or grabbing a sweet treat and texting a friend to let you know you've aced another chunk of revision. Knowing you've done something well brings its own '**intrinsic**' rewards — that feeling of personal achievement inside — but it's good to celebrate your mini-successes with '**extrinsic**' rewards too — like enjoying a nice chunky slab of cake!

Making yourself responsible for what you do is powerful. It's not easy for those you live with either; they'd much rather you could do what you wanted, but both you and they want the best for you. This also isn't about telling your family that you don't deserve a break . . .

BANISHING PROCRASTINATION IS ABOUT ENSURING THAT WHEN YOU'RE 'ON IT', YOU REALLY ARE 'ON IT'.

19

USE YOUR ARMY OF HELP

If you say, 'Mum, I have no self-control. Please could you hide my phone for an hour while I revise?' — you are not admitting defeat. You are enlisting someone from your trusted **battalion** of helpers, who are going to be really important in getting you through the revision period.

They aren't there to lock your bedroom door and chain you to your desk so that you revise, but they are there to cajole, persuade, praise, commiserate, cheer, laugh and cry with. We've already talked about how hard you'll be working throughout this time, but when you have a moment to think, the emotional side of it can be absolutely exhausting.

And your army doesn't just stop at your front door. It extends to your pals, your peers, your teachers, your form tutor. They're all going through their own experiences of these exams, but they're all in your corner, absolutely and unashamedly desperate for you to succeed.

Social support has an active effect on the brain, and many studies have shown that having the right people around you reduces anxiety and depression and can enhance wellbeing. So ready those recruits, sir, yes sir!

SERIOUS SERGEANT MAJOR

Who do you need to have a right go at you when you're just not doing what you should? Is it your grandma who you're truly terrified of and don't want to let down? Tell her what you need from her — she could be your pep talk queen when you're not quite doing what you should be.

REVISION REGIMENT

Whoever you live with, this is probably going to be them. You'd be surprised how useful your mum, dad, step-mum, sister, guardian or whoever else you share your house with can be. While they're not sitting in your lessons with you, and they won't be doing your exams with you, giving them jobs along the way can make your life so much easier. Assign them some roles.

CHIEF QUIZMASTER

They'll start to do your head in, but that's good. Give them your flash cards and they instantly transform into Ant and/or Dec, asking questions until you win a fancy holiday (actually not a fancy holiday — more like a slightly more developed understanding of binary for your computer science paper). Aim to help them understand what you need to know — that shows that you're able to communicate what you know clearly and effectively. That's what an examiner is looking for you to do.

BREAK BATTALION

You've planned in breaks and rewards, and you need to take them. If you're in the zone, there's a good chance you'll try and say, 'Oh, but just an hour more . . . ' But what's planned is planned (unless, of course, you need a last-minute change). This role is an important one, in that they're the person who sits you down, gets you a cup of tea and gets your head out of revision for a short time. They don't have an easy ride — they're responsible for helping you keep your revision healthy.

SUSTENANCE SQUADRON

Food and drink are important for everyone; we all know that. But for you, in the middle of your exam schedule, eating well, regularly and healthily is critical. When you're tired and busy, it's easy to be tempted to smash junk food directly into your mouth or see a bag of sugary sweets as an ideal lunch.

Eating poorly leads to your blood sugar (and your energy) going in peaks and troughs, meaning that you might feel amazing after a bar of chocolate for breakfast, but pretty soon your blood sugar will nosedive and you'll feel devoid of energy. Regular water, fruit, vegetables and keeping a healthy, balanced diet will make a huge difference to how you feel (and how you perform before and during your exams).

If you struggle to stay on that right track when it comes to sustenance, rope in your parents or siblings to help you keep on the straight and narrow.

COMEDY COMRADE

This one's important, too. **Despite the fact life is busy, you need to keep a sense of perspective.** When things go wrong, it's important to plan so they don't go wrong again, but it's also OK to bounce the daft thing you did off someone else so that one of three things happens:

- You realise it's not as bad as you thought
- You realise that you're not the only one (as plenty of others will have done the same)
- You have a good old laugh about it

Laughter boosts your intake of oxygen, increases the endorphins released by the brain, **lowers stress** hormones and can relax your whole body. So, find your comedy comrade, that one person who you can let off a bit of steam with and **have a good old laugh!**

CHIEF COUNSELLOR

Whether it's a hug from your mum, a cry across the table from your cousin or a snotty outburst into your grandpa's jumper which leads to a dry-cleaning bill, **this is the job that the people who love you are best at**. They're there for you, so use them to counsel you. Ask questions, offload your worries and be honest. You will rarely regret making the decision to share your problems. Adults have often seen loads of this stuff too, so there's a pretty excellent chance you won't just offload . . . you'll pick up some useful tips.

SO, STAND TO ATTENNNSHUN!

THE SUPPORT SQUADRON'S READY AND WAITING. BELIEVE ME WHEN I SAY THEY'RE ITCHING TO HELP YOU. GET THOSE ROLES ASSIGNED AND USE THEM TO PROPEL YOU TO VICTORY IN THIS BATTLE TO THAT FINAL EXAM!

20

QUICK
FIXES

The aeroplane is descending and the cabin crew have been told to take their seats for landing. You've heard the clank of the wheels coming down and you can see the sea from your window. The exam runway is flashing into view – and you've furiously flicked through to this chapter because you realise that everyone else has started and you haven't even thought about what's to come yet.

If this is you, don't panic.

Whether there's a month left or — shock horror! — a week, there are still things you can do. We're going to keep exam season flying smoothly and touch down in style.

PRIORITISE

Make a to-do list with priority labels next to each item and a timeframe for when to complete them. That way, you will see exactly what's most important. For example:

- **Plot points in *The Tempest***
  – super-urgent : complete this morning

- **Atomic structures**
  – important : complete this evening

- **Coastal erosion**
  – low-priority: complete tomorrow

MAKE-A-DIFFERENCE MATRIX

While every bit of knowledge that might be examined is important, there are certain parts which are likely to come up more than others or are worth more marks. These have higher impact. At this point, it makes more sense to prioritise those and try to bank as many marks as possible. If you're not sure where to start, ask your teacher, as they might have a steer. Then try plotting out where subjects fall on a 'make-a-difference matrix'.

Focus on the things you can do that have the highest impact and require the lowest effort first, then move to things that have high impact but require a bit more time. Things in the bottom left can be done later, and for things that have a low impact but take high effort, rethink whether this is the right time to do them at all.

High impact

French verbs flash cards	Algebraic formulae
Do this NOW	**Do this NEXT**

Low effort ←--------------→ **High effort**

Do this LATER	**DON'T DO THIS**
Human body and movement	Anything irrelevant to looming exams

Low impact

DON'T STAY UP ALL NIGHT

You might be tempted to start pulling all-nighters at this point, but doing so will only make things worse. Lack of sleep actually has the OPPOSITE effect to what you want. It will stop memories from being laid down, and all that last-minute cramming will be in vain. Not only that, being tired reduces performance the next day.

There comes a point where you have to stop cramming and get some shut-eye, and that is earlier in the evening than you think. Quality sleep is scientifically proven to help you solve problems. Sometimes if you can't quite get that revision down, you literally do need to sleep on it!

CONTROL WHAT YOU CAN

In your exams, just like in life, there are things that you can control and things you can't. At this point, you can control how hard you work, how seriously you take the next few days or weeks and what happens from this point. Whether you come out with top grades or not, you can certainly do everything within your power from this point to make yourself, and your loved ones, proud as punch.

EVEN THOUGH IT MIGHT BE LATER THAN YOU'D HOPED, YOU'VE GOT A REASON AND A PLAN. GO AND ACE IT.

PART THREE

ACE YOUR EXAMS

Nerves are normal. Let's not pretend they're not. But you're ready for this. You've worked, you've revised, you've covered your entire house in flash cards and mind maps to the point where even your baby sister can confidently write a 90-word French essay about her holidays now.

You've got it, you know it. But how's that day going to feel, and how are you going to cope with the seemingly relentless cycle of exams, revision, school and study leave? Well let's have a think about it. Dive in!

21

APPROACHING THE BIG DAY

So here we are. Exams are here. It isn't a shock to you (or at least it shouldn't be) and it's what you've been working so hard for. You've done so much work, it's time to approach the big day right.

EAT HEALTHY

Your brain needs you to stay healthy now more than ever. Eating a healthy, balanced diet, full of veggies and nutrient-packed food, will do that brain of yours wonders. Foods with omega-3, such as oily fish like mackerel, or soybeans and walnuts, are going to actively enhance blood flow in the brain and help with your memory.

Keeping yourself hydrated is going to keep your brain alert as well.

PERFECT PREP

The night before your exam, make sure you:

- Have the equipment you need packed and ready to go
- Set your alarm
- Go to bed on time — no last-minute staying up all night cramming

You also need to know how you're getting to school the next day. Is it business as usual, or do you have to be earlier or later? Do you have a back-up plan if something goes wrong? Arriving flustered, because you set off late doesn't help you. Having an extra fifteen minutes waiting around at school to have a last look over your notes is a much better thing to do than sweating and panicking and realising the exam started ten minutes ago and your bus hasn't turned up.

STAY CALM

Pretty soon you'll be in the exam hall. It's an environment that you'll know from all the practices you've done and probably all the PE lessons you've done in there over the last few years. But there is a difference when it's the 'real' thing. You might feel an added tension, knowing that everyone else in schools up and down the country is doing that same paper, at the same time, and they are all racing for the same grades. If your mind is racing, use the breathing techniques you've learnt to calm it down.

FOLLOW THE RULES

What you absolutely must do on the day of each exam is follow every single rule. The rules are in place to make sure that exams are done fairly and so that nobody is disadvantaged or given special treatment.

If you're told to hand over your watch, your phone, your tablet, your revision guides or any notes you've made, make sure you do. You need to make sure that you have nothing in the exam which has any writing on it, so that it's fair and clear for everyone. If you've brought your own pencil case in, check it's a clear one and that it doesn't have a load of revision notes stuffed down the lining which you forgot to take out.

There might be a sneaking thought to yourself that it doesn't really matter. That nobody will check. Well, let me tell you two things: yes it does, and yes they will. The alternative isn't really something you want to think about, but if you're caught with something which you're not allowed in an exam, you could lose some or all the marks in the paper, or you could have all your exams made null and void. That wouldn't be a good end to a period of your life you've dedicated so much to.

If you're in the exam and in the heat of the moment you remember you have something in your pocket you shouldn't, then pop your hand up and tell someone. Honest mistakes happen; people understand that.

CHECK AND CHECK AGAIN

Another potential exam paper pitfall is a simple one. You must **always check that the subject, date, title of the paper and the tier of entry are right**. Although everyone tries to get everything right, mistakes happen, and this means that examiners make them too. If you think you're going in to sit a Spanish exam and the paper says 'Biology' on it, something's gone wrong. Again, pop your hand up and someone will sort it.

And finally, before you open the cover and start scribbling, the front of the paper gives you some 'advice' — often it's under a heading saying that you 'could' spend certain amounts of time on certain sections, and it helps with the tactics of attacking the next two hours. Don't read 'could' — read it as 'should'. **It's there to help you, so use it.**

AND WITH THAT, IT'S ABOUT TIME TO OPEN THE FRONT COVER AND CRACK ON. SHALL WE?

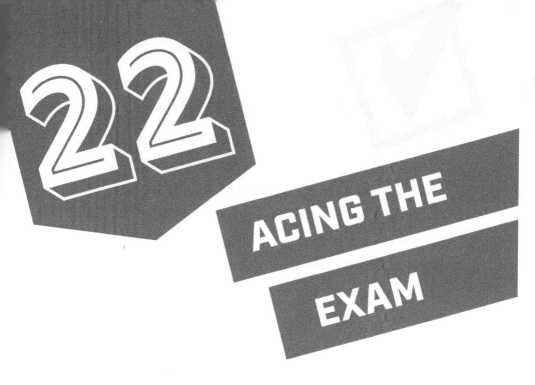

ACING THE EXAM

If things have gone well and your revision has done what it's supposed to have done, you'll quickly realise that you've nothing to be scared of. Mostly, people are worried about not doing well, but it sort of becomes enjoyable when you realise you've **revised** the right stuff and you're feeling good about showing what you know.

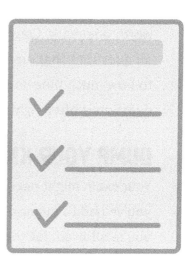

Still, a few handy hints to help along the way wouldn't go amiss, would they?

READ EVERY QUESTION TWICE

This might seem a bit daft, but make sure you read the question and then go back and read it again. There'd be nothing worse than spending an hour on 'the causes of the Second World War' when actually the question asked for the 'consequences' of the Second World War. Highlight the absolute KEY things the question is asking you for, and make sure you understand what is expected of you before you begin.

LOOK AT THE MARKS ON OFFER

Don't spend hours and hours on questions that are just worth one mark. Conversely, don't spend just five minutes on questions that are worth twenty. A great, rough guide to how much time you should be spending on each question is often right in front of you. So don't miss it.

DUMP YOUR KNOWLEDGE

Your exam might need quotes, formulae or equations that you've had to memorise. You absolutely can, as soon as you're allowed, jot them down on a piece of scrap paper and keep it to one side. If a quote is a bit tricky or you know you're struggling to remember this formula or that fact, dump it out of your brain straight away.

SAY BYE-BYE TO BLANK SPACE

This isn't a criticism of Taylor Swift, so please don't come at me if you're a Swiftie. I just don't like blank space being left in exams. So I'll make this simple: DO NOT LEAVE ANY QUESTION UNANSWERED!

If your timings go amiss, write as much as you can in the time you've got. If you genuinely do not know the answer, take a guess. Get something down. Something's better than nothing, and a sensible guess might actually be somewhere near right!

TIME CHECKS

You'll be able to see clocks in the hall which are super clear about the time, and what time the exam finishes. Check the clocks and keep your pace where it should be. Not rushing, but also not spending forever on a question that is only worth a couple of marks.

USE YOUR EQUIPMENT

Your brain and your hands are your main equipment, but there's also space for highlighters, calculators (in some exams), copies of books (in some exams) and source material such as case studies or the periodic table (again, in some exams).

KEEP SCHTUM AND DO YOUR BIT

Everyone deserves to have an exam hall where they can concentrate on doing their best, and you play an important role in making and maintaining that environment. Be quiet. If you need the loo, put your hand up. If you need to ask a question? Same again – hand up. If you feel poorly, do the same. It's not that communication with the invigilators is banned – they're there to help – but it needs to be done in a way that keeps things lovely and calm. Anyone who's chatting or communicating in an exam can end up with serious problems – exam marks can be cancelled, and that's not good for anyone at all.

PUT IT TO BED

When it's done, it's done. Nothing can change when that exam's over. It might have been amazing or disastrous, but that affects nothing in your next one. Put a line through it on your timetable and move on to the next one. The system you've got – your plan, habits and process – are sustainable. Don't over-analyse everything, because you need that energy for the next exam. If physics was a failure, English could still be exceptional and French could be fabulous.

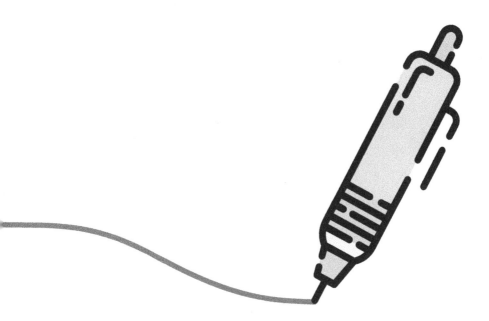

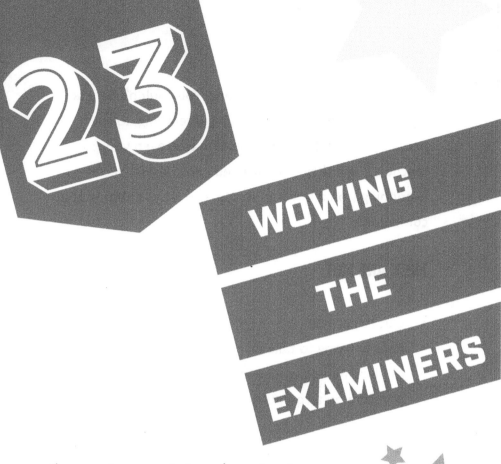

23

WOWING THE EXAMINERS

I'm sure, in your mind, you've got a clear picture of what you think an examiner looks like. You might think they'd be a retired teacher who enjoys finding opportunities to scratch a huge red 'X' across a paper and generally wants you to fail spectacularly. They possibly even seek out your paper in particular just to make your life a misery, so that they can give you zero marks.

Well, you'd be wrong. Bang wrong. You couldn't be less right. Examiners are normal, living, breathing, lovely people. Usually they're teachers (maybe even your teachers), and they don't use red pens (insider secret – everything's on a screen nowadays so they're staring at a computer)!

THEY ARE NOT:

- Out to get you
- Able or trying to take marks away from you
- Marking named work – most papers will be marked by question on a computer screen and anonymised

THEY ARE:

- Teachers
- Looking to award marks wherever they can
- Keen to see papers that are clear, easy to mark and done well

But how do you WOW them? Well, I can't cover specifics about Arabic and algebra in detail, and flitting between food technology and physics wouldn't help, but this one-stop shop for exam advice will help get you on their good side and will help in every single one, whether it's biology or basket weaving.

FOLLOW THE RULES ON THE FRONT AND GET THE BASICS RIGHT!

This is a big area that can please (or upset) examiners. They settle down, make a lovely cup of tea, decide they're going to start marking by clicking on your exam. It's been a long day at work and they're really excited to read a cracking exam answer . . . AND THE ANSWERS AREN'T NUMBERED! The front of the paper will have some really clear rules on — stuff about writing certain details and (sometimes) signing it. It'll tell you how to set questions out, how many to pick, and what to do if you run out of room. Give yourself the best chance of getting the credit for the work you've done so much towards by making sure it's all clearly completed (and writing with a blue or black pen).

WRITE NEATLY

One of the most avoidable errors people make when doing their exams is making it really difficult to read, maybe through rushing, or panicking, or carelessness. If it's tough to read, it's tough to mark.

IF IT'S TOUGH TO MARK, IT'S TOUGH TO GIVE YOU ANY SCORE FOR IT.

If you think that your handwriting is a problem you might struggle with, talk to school. If it's something that your school is aware of, there might be a chance for you to type your answers instead of writing them through something called 'access arrangements' (which is when people get a bit of extra support when it's needed).

ANSWER THE ACTUAL QUESTION

Take a breath, read the question and write what you know about it. You'll only get marks for the answers the examiners are looking for, so it's better to write about a really precise answer about what's being asked for, rather than ramble on and on for pages about stuff that isn't relevant. **Answer. The. Question!**

DON'T GIVE UP

There may be frustrating papers that you just can't seem to do, but keep persevering. Make sure that you've done everything you can. Ask yourself these three questions:

Did I work to the end?
Was it challenging?
Did I do everything I could?

IF THE ANSWER TO ALL THREE IS YES, THEN IT'S LIKELY TO HAVE GONE WELL. IF YOU DID EVERYTHING YOU COULD (BOTH AT HOME AND IN THE EXAM), THEN THAT'S ALL YOU CAN DO.

24

BEATING BACK-TO-BACK EXAMS

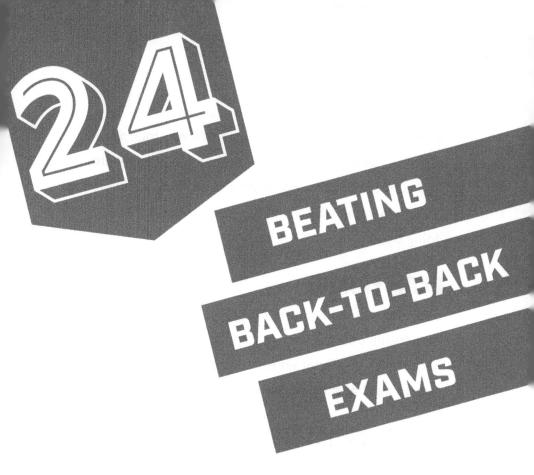

Once things get going, you'll be in a completely new routine of eat, sleep, revise, exam, repeat. It might feel really weird, but at this stage, keeping your **discipline** and routine are the **name of the game**.

The nerves of the first exam will soon be gone, and you'll be into the relentless cycle of back-to-back exams for a few weeks. At this point there are a few risks that you want to avoid.

OVERCONFIDENCE

One or two exams going well doesn't mean they all will, especially without the hard work that needs to go with it. Overconfidence can come from a good thing – confidence – but remember why things have gone well and keep doing them.

EXAM FATIGUE

Every exam is worth something, but it can be far too easy to slip into feeling like some are less important because it's 'just another one'. It'll be a tiring period, but remember that they all deserve the same level of respect.

CATASTROPHISING

You'll come out of one or two exams and talk to your friends about how they found it. You might realise that you've made some silly mistakes and be really annoyed with yourself. Some people then wrongly think there's no point any more. Think about the number of questions you'll be answering across the summer – hundreds and hundreds of them. One or two being wrong isn't too bad, is it?!

RUSHING THROUGH

Yes, you want to get through to the end. It's been a long, long road to get to this point, but make the most of it.

GIVE EVERY EXAM THE TIME AND ATTENTION IT NEEDS, OTHERWISE YOU WILL REGRET IT.

This is all about pacing yourself and keeping things as normal as possible in perhaps the least normal time of your life.

As well as avoiding these risks, there are some things that you absolutely should do:

KEEP IN CONTACT WITH PEOPLE

Your friends are going through the same thing as you and probably feel as strange about the weird freedom – which isn't really freedom! – you're in. Talk to them and maybe even do some paired revision. We've already talked about halving problems by sharing them – keep doing it.

CHECK IN ON YOUR MIND

This is stressful, there's no doubt about it. You'll constantly feel like you should be doing something, even when you really need to be resting.

KEEP TICKING OVER WITH THE MEDITATION AND EXERCISES FOR YOUR MENTAL HEALTH.

FUEL UP

Don't skip meals. Keep drinking. You might not be running 26.2 miles every day, but your schedule is punishing. You're running a mental marathon while your exams are on, and to do that you need fuel in your system.

STICK WITH IT

Don't let procrastination ruin your chances of success. No arranging your glass bottle collection into size order and then individually polishing the knives and forks in the cutlery drawer. If you want to do things, just WAIT A FEW WEEKS!

STICK TO THE ROUTINE THAT'S PUT YOU WITHIN TOUCHING DISTANCE OF SUPER SUCCESS!

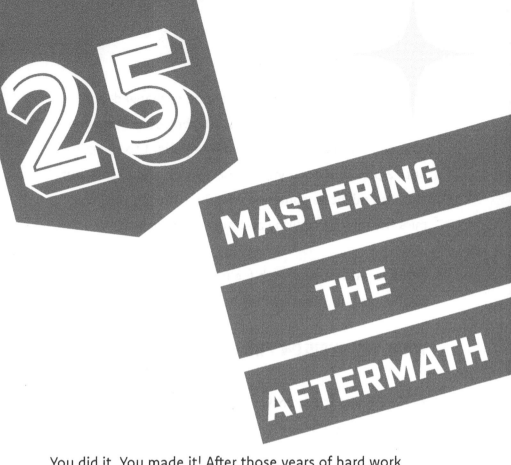

25 MASTERING THE AFTERMATH

You did it. You made it! After those years of hard work and routines, you will step out of your final exam into the warm summer air, and you'll feel . . . a bit strange.

School becomes a huge part of most people's lives. We all complain about some parts of it, and lots of happy and sad tears are set against the backdrop of friendships, fallouts, detentions, homework, break times, school dinners and lessons . . . And despite the fact it's great to have a seemingly endless summer stretching out far into the distance, you can feel a bit numb.

Shirts might be signed, hugs might be exchanged, and some tears might even be shed. Maybe you're someone who can't wait to get away and is impatient to sleep in until 2 p.m. and do anything but revision and exams, but you also might be someone who, in a strange way, will miss the intense scrutiny and buzz of exam season.

Either is natural, and both feelings are normal. Most people probably feel a bit of both.

WHAT YOU SHOULDN'T DO NOW IS:

- Stress about the answers your mates gave if you wrote something different
- Forget all the good stuff you've done and the way you've worked towards a goal
- Panic about how the exams have gone

But, equally, when that moment arrives, there are some things that you really should do. I can't tell you what they are, because they are the things you like. Pottery, paintball, paddling, pool, ping-pong. This period now is all about you, but in a different way to before your final exam kicked off.

You have literally no way of knowing how things have gone until you get to that fateful day in August, but you'll have a decent sense of things based on those three questions we mentioned before, which you can ask yourself after every exam.

It can feel a bit strange going from being really busy to having some time off. After the euphoria of being done with exams, some people feel a bit lacking in motivation.

Try planning your time, making memories with friends, or even looking ahead to your course next year and getting ahead of the game. It can help to have a bit of structure as well as downtime.

If you've affected what you can affect, if you've worked hard, then you can rest easy. Know that you could not have done more.

At some point in the first week after your last exam, it's useful to spend an hour reflecting on the achievements you've unlocked over the last few weeks. It's better to do it when the exams are over but before you find out how you've done, because you can reflect on the process, rather than the outcome.

THINK ABOUT:

- ## WHAT YOU FOUND MOST DIFFICULT
- ## WHAT WORKED FOR YOU
- ## HOW YOU BEST AVOIDED GETTING DISTRACTED
- ## HOW WORKING HARD MADE YOU FEEL
- ## HOW IT FELT WHEN YOU DIDN'T WORK AS HARD AS YOU SHOULD HAVE
- ## WHAT YOU'RE MOST PROUD OF

Pushing the question of your outcomes to the back of your mind is easier said than done, but time does help. You probably won't be able to do it immediately after your final exam, but over the next week, when you're sleeping in a bit, relaxing with friends and family more than you have been, and maybe even doing a bit of part-time work, your thoughts will quickly turn to other things.

It's important that you gave it everything, but now it's important you give yourself a break. You've worked, you've revised, you've executed your game plan. Now go get yourself a pizza, get those feet up on the sofa and put a film on. Lay back and say with me, 'Ahhhh'. Even have a nap, if you want. Let your mind wander to this time last week, when you were just starting that final paper.

RELAX. WELL DONE. YOU'VE EARNED IT.

EPILOGUE: RESULTS DAY

Seems a while ago, doesn't it? That moment of writing the date down in the first lesson all those months ago, thinking, worrying and drifting off in your mind to that place where you would eventually be stepping into an exam . . . and trying to ace it.

Well, you did it. Yes, you had a hand from some top teachers, properly good parents and fantastic friends, but it was **you**.

Only one person can open that envelope at the end of the summer, and you know who that is. Whatever's in there doesn't define you, but if it's great, it's really helpful. If it's not, you'll be able to have another go.

However things have gone, you should be proud. It's a lot to do; it's a massive amount of hard work and rewiring your brain from that small child who started secondary school a few years ago into this sophisticated young adult who's aced their exams.

You've dealt with the highs and lows, the disappointments and the happiness, and you've battled through some really difficult, rock-hard work and come out the other side.

Be proud, whatever the outcome. Look at what you can do now that you couldn't do before you started your exams, and spend some time thinking about the person you are now compared to back then. You might feel like a different person altogether, and that would be absolutely right.

THERE'LL BE CHALLENGES AHEAD, SO LET'S REFOCUS. SHIFT YOUR GAZE TO THE NEXT GOAL, WHICH IS STILL BUILDING TOWARDS THAT VISION OF SUCCESS IN THE FUTURE.

Write it down and lock it away. That won't change, even if those grades aren't as good as you'd like. You'll have other periods in your life — maybe even in a couple of years' time — when you have to do a similar thing, but even as you get into your career in the future, these are all bits of your character you'll need to be able to show.

There are few points in a human life that will be quite as stressful, as tough and as mentally challenging as doing your exams.

YOU'VE DONE THAT.
CONGRATULATIONS.

SMILE.
YOU
ACED IT!

RESOURCES

BBC Bitesize

A free online resource to help with homework, learning and revision.

www.bbc.co.uk/bitesize/learn

Mind

Mind is a mental health charity. In the link below you can find information about how to deal with the stresses of exams and revision.

www.mind.org.uk/for-young-people/feelings-and-experiences/tips-for-coping-with-exam-stress/

Childline

A counselling service for children and young people. Their website has lots of advice, articles and games to help with mental health and exam preparation.

www.childline.org.uk/info-advice/school-college-and-work/school-college/homework-revision/

ALSO BY MATTHEW BURTON